The Cure

Also by Sarah Gorham

poetry

The Tension Zone

Don't Go Back to Sleep

The Night Lifted Us (with Jeffrey Skinner)

anthologies

Last Call: Poems on Alcoholism, Addiction, and Deliverance (ed. with Jeffrey Skinner)

The Cure

Sarah Gorham

Four Way Books
New York City

Distributed by
University Press of New England
Hanover and London

Editorial Office
Four Way Books
POB 535, Village Station
New York, NY 10014
www.fourwaybooks.com

Library of Congress Catalogue Card Number: 2002116852

ISBN 1-884800-51-3

Cover painting: Eric Fischl, "Communion," 1997. Reproduced by kind permission of the artist.

This book is manufactured in the United States of America and printed on acid-free paper.

Four Way Books is a division of Friends of Writers, Inc., a Vermont-based not-for-profit organization. We are grateful for the assistance we receive from individual donors and private foundations.

Distributed by University Press of New England
One Court Street, Lebanon, NH 03766

ACKNOWLEDGMENTS

Agni: "Half Empty/Half Full," "Watch Your Language"
American Poetry Review: "Icon," "The Minor Stations,"
    "Cupped Ear"
Controlled Burn: "Playing for Robert McNamara"
DoubleTake: "Coda, in Winter" under the title "Winter Love
    Poem"
Gettysburg Review: "Sleeping on Couches"
Georgia Review: "Nothing Human"
The Journal: "Keying Down," "Honeymoon, Pleasant Hill"
Michigan Quarterly Review: "Love Thy Neighbor"
The Ohio Review: "Interim"
Open City: "Bacchus at The Water Tower," "Middle Age"
The Paris Review: "Shared Cup," "Cupped Hands"
Poetry East: "River Mild"
Passages North: "Scotoma"
Prairie Schooner: "Shot Glass," "Spilled Cup," "Derby
    Glass," "Champagne Flute"
Southern Review: "Succession," "Daughter's Villanelle,"
    "The Cure," "Crossing Myself," "Retreat"

"Shot Glass," "Spilled Cup," "Derby Glass," and
    "Champagne Flute" won *Prairie Schooner*'s 2000
    Reader's Choice Award.

"Dear Growing Teen" appeared in *Teaching the Art of
    Poetry*, by Baron Wormser and Robert Cappella.

"River Mild" was reprinted in *Who Are the Rich and Where
    Do They Live?* edited by Richard Jones.

Jeffrey, again.
And my girls, Laura and Bonnie.

CONTENTS

I.

II.

III.

Why do you wash the outside of the cup? Don't you understand that the maker of the outside also made the inside?

– *The Logia of Yeshua*

I.

Interim

She loves the subway caught between stations.
A butcher fanning himself with the sports section.
A child's chlorinated hair whorled in a tight nest.
She wants that face-to-face with a stranger's
boredom, flat and unsmiling.

Or in the late afternoon, the pause
for delicious heat, draped over the city
like a cashmere glove. She eavesdrops,
tunes in housewives for their coping cliches:
One day at a time. Live and let live—
like those dream steering wheels
that float in your hands.

Once, she kissed a stranger's ironed sleeve
merely to be outside, to feel his scent replace her own.
With age, she thought, we know ourselves
better, *yes,* our lives rising
around us like a mirrored bowl. What she wants

is a moment of *unknowing;*
she wants to be a rose, pressed between the pages
of someone else's story.

Half Empty/Half Full

Reasons to grieve: diminishing flesh,
weeks that scroll by unnoticed.
Coarseness of image and voice.
Rain of ash on Montseurrat,
milkweed that loosens in a sudden gale.
The mirrored hall of adolescence,
rootlessness of politicians.
Books that end up in the air, seas
that pare away the shore. The black horse,
black horse that throws its rider.
The sinking of foundations and moral standards.
Blur of small print, medicine that comes too late.
The reduction of great literary characters
to one or two dismissive sentences.
Pale skin, cold coffee,
wandering attention. Unpainted boats.

Reasons to rejoice: skin closing
after an abrasion. First attenuated hours
of vacation. Swell of rivers
and waves and the White Mountains.
Simple accounts: *I'm relieved. I'm first in line.*
The red hot blaze before the ash, milkweed
feathering down. The transformation of sisters
into late-life companions.
Fresh sheets, a bar of glycerine soap.
Open-ended novels. Tram tickets, tea time,
little red spiders, the other minutiae
behind great open-ended novels.
Aspirin that prevents, caresses that sway,
primer to hold the bright coat of paint.
Aphorisms, epigrams, succinct parables:

Two horses fighting, one black, one white.
Which horse will win?
The one you feed the most.
Again: the one you feed the most.

Bacchus at The Water Tower, Continuing Ed

We gather this was homework: *Mix the godly*
with the mundane. Paint some place
you know. The tower is 1890s
Greek Revival, and Bacchus looms in front
with purple lips and wandering
bloodshot eye. There's plenty of drapery,
including a cement-colored toga
sheathing the left half of his body.
The artist didn't have to paint another arm,
and good thing, for the naked one's yellow
and lumpy like coffee cake. Our God of Libation
is showing repercussions of excess,
a hepatic glow spreading up his chest and neck
though the warning we guess is unintentional—
our artist "Spike" proclaims in all caps
on onion skin that he himself
"loves the application of paint to canvas..."
it is a *"sensual process"* for him.
How charming in late life
this second look at profit-sharing
and I-beam manufacturing
which we gather from his
shaky signature has damaged more
than our good friend's spirit.
He's following the whiff of long-ago pleasure
and, amazingly, hasn't hurt anyone.
Except Bacchus perhaps, who looks distressed.
Some afterlife, he thinks and would bolt
right off the canvas, if only his creator
had left him a proper skeleton.
It's as if the boy survived the lightning blast
only to miss the reconstruction,
nestled inside his father's shapely thigh.
Spike has an inkling of this lack

but unlike his subject he's no lush—
a practical man who enrolled in 'studio classes,'
and hopes to "pursue his masters at U of L."
In closing, the slightest flicker from his past:
"I truly enjoy the process,
and I hope you enjoy the product."
Sealed with a fire-engine red, nickle-sized price tag.
Eighty bucks. A real bargain.

Love Thy Neighbor

Two fingers creaky and stiff
I could chalk up to
pitting cherries for an hour.

But, the next day hurts too
and then all of my fingers,
typing as if I wore
mittens made of dough.

Someone must have seen me
curse Mr. Mulzer
(Wake up Mr. Mulzer. Hello?)
who chose my harried path
to block with his walker, thought

*she could use a
sympathy implant—
a little early arthritis...*

For now I see the difficulty
in easy chairs
and insert-knife-here
vacuum wrap. Psychologists

just don't get it,
proximity no guarantee
of good will—

it's got to be personal,
my swollen knuckle
younger cousin
to his frozen limbs.

Sweet, verkachte Mr. Mulzer.
He's my hero now
for sticking to his routine:
shuffle to the Food Mart,
buy the paper, bring it home.

Succession

We are flying inside the storm, rain
stretched taut against the windows like piano wire.
We are turning, though it seems the clouds themselves
circle us, bandaging with their white gauze.
Our belts are secure. Hands do not fly
into our neighbor's faces.
The attendant keeps our cups filled
bracing herself with a knee.
We set our watches ahead.

                               Listen to her,
telling us to remain seated, calm,
to make the sky our home, ride with it
like a flea on the back of a cow.
Our carry-ons fall. Sunglasses shimmy
across our faces, but why not believe her—
she is our guide and well-spoken
and her tiny guest pillows feel honest
against our spines. We lean forward
as she folds the flannel blankets, stashes them
out of reach. Soon she will slip away.

So too the houses and fields below,
like clothes we've suddenly outgrown,
passed on to younger sisters.

Spilled Cup

She likes to catch her mother
off guard. Sure thing—
clatter against plate,
mother's rush with hands open
then back to grab a waffle cloth.
The milk traces a swollen line
across table, down tooled leg
to linoleum, trim, and now
the little one gleefully
splashes in the stuff—gray
where once there was ruled
black and white. Her dad
laid the cement himself
and mealtimes, there's no hiding
the room's flaws. Everybody knows—
you can't spoil a baby but
my, how this baby
has spoiled them.
Upended their insides
so that all is a mix of mean
and flirty, morning and night.
Sometimes they hardly speak
for what might be
accidentally confessed.

Playing for Robert McNamara

Surely there were other guests
but I remember only McNamara,
his hair lathered and smooth,
skull shining through.
My father stroked him, 100% charm,
while mother blurred between kitchen
and chair. Her tight, gracious conversation,
her machine gun laugh;
a sudden surge of chairs as she fell
tossing spoons and a platter
of tapioca and cream.
Our new Indian tablecloth. Oh well.

McNamara was coaxed with coffee
into the living room. *Sarah is taking lessons*,
my mother explained,
Play something for us, Sarah dear.
And I chose the piece I knew well,
Little Prelude in C, because
it made me sound professional,
though I fumbled the left hand entrance
and had to start again.
(March on! said Mrs. Jacobsen.)
McNamara clapped, which I liked a lot
and so, hung around a beat too long.

Sarah, go play a game.
Or something.... Mother glared.
McNamara looked uncomfortable
and scooped up our cat in his giant
hands, murmuring low.
My sisters snickered behind the door—
we were on our best behavior.
Later, we tore each other's dresses
and pulled each other's hair.

In Waiting, ICU

Big sister folds giftwrap
into an angular swan.
Middle one paces the hall.
I ring the nurse's bell

at fifteen minute intervals.
Then Nancy with her
vase of purple tulips...

Their ice shifts.
The patient cheers.

What's the plan here?
I have to know. Once
they rested in peace—

now the dying instruct us.
My mother taps twice
for yes, one time for no
till I know to find

the gift shop,
the perfect slippers.
Her toes are blue with cold.
My purchase

isn't charity so much
as one last hope
she'll notice,
and love me, alone.

Icon

The carved wooden baby
has a mature man's face,
a likeness, you're guessing,
of the artist himself.

His halo is veneered
gold leaf. Unclear
what's underneath.
But in case you were tempted

to think the portrait
beyond place, the painted stars
are really a map
of fifteenth century Barcelona.

The well rendered hair
is chiseled, then scrafittoed
in the ancient fashion
as the ringlets of his followers

bear witness. And the hand
sweeps East, rearranging
the natural order, though the chosen
are still poor, still suffering.

Think well of yourself
who value reason and equanimity,
who pity the baby its small,
necessary death.

Retreat

Monk says they were moved here from France—
grave markers jumbled together like a yard sale.
One's a squiggle of iron, another imbedded with glass.
The fanciest sits on a diagonal—
curvaceous, like a perfume bottle. Salmon and lavender
dahlias but the real flower's months away in another town
since nothing like that grows around here.
Meanwhile it's Christmastime near the plainest stone
where cedar and bows teeter on a wire easel.
Where are the relatives? Are the bodies in Antibes?
Perhaps my gaze is too static, or close
but I want something in sync: native plants, tinsel
in season, and one man dressed in robes
who isn't dreaming of someplace else.

Lullaby on Your Own

Your mother is alive and well
in Portugal. She sends you
a crisp day, an exceptional
honeybelle, green lights
all the way home.

Your mother is flying above your car
silently like a high altitude jet.
She watches while you slow,
unstrap your belt, nuzzle the dog,
lie down.

Your mother keeps the bad news
in her cliptop purse
tucked between two Kleenexes.
She holds back traffic, hunger;
she gives that deadline another week.

Your mother doesn't care
that you are an excitable boss,
a worrier, an uneven mother.
She loves your hair
and the bump on your thumb.

Your mother cups her hands
over the hall light and hums.
Slipping away, she coaxes a poem
from inside you, the two repeating words
like matching pillows.

Nothing Human

– after Jeanne Dueber's "Angel"

Close up there are no human features
only geological ones
as if the angel were cut from a hill
where water gushed and crayfish
fossilized. Or perhaps these bumps and jags
and troughs are indeed anatomical,
a magnified three-inch triangle of flesh—
nowhere a discernible eye, hand, mouth.
Why shouldn't it be like this,

the idealized version with wings
a sad and arrogant dream
rising obediently to comfort us
the moment we breathe the word "God."
The spirit begins in texture and disorder,
as in the onset of our own bodies:
an angel like a bud of femur,
an angel like a drop of blood.
This is what accompanies us,

and what we deserve
after our hurried prayers.
We must pray more often.
Prayer is a backing away from the self.
When we step away from the sculpture,
there's a curious softness to its middle,
a gentle dip on the left.
Nothing human, for we are still
too human. Nothing peaceful.

We are impatient, and return
to touch it with our blunt hands.

Vanitas for a Doomed Affair

Two pears on a branch
nestle cheek to cheek.
They droop heavily to the ground
where an animal we cannot see
has nibbled an irregular bite.
It mirrors the jagged hole
in a terracotta vase,
lifted and nearly shattered.
How could anyone trust again?
On the vase is a swan,
its neck a tiny hook
without a fish. Another swan
lingers nearby, its
curving body a question
for which there was an answer
though not the one we'd like.
And the rose,
like an upside-down dress,
and the cantaloupe, sliced open
upon the table.
And the ring in a ceramic dish.
Was it always in the dish,
or, during her unhappy search,
hidden, hushed
in his satin-lined pocket?

Rebound Tenderness

With an abrupt jolt
her lover let up his insistence.
No more name-calling,
no more poking and prodding.
He drew back, and was gone.

For years, she'd been opaque,
cool like an ice lens
under his touch. Presto,
she's flooded with color,
anger and blame,
her body's final attempt
to heal up the rent.

It's a classic symptom—pain
when the pressure is released.
Doctors call it "rebound tenderness"
and in tenderness lies the cure
for her unstable condition.

Or so said the 17th century surgeon,
Wilhelm Hilden.
Everyone thought he was a fool,
applying his medicine to the knife
instead of the wound.
To heal, she must relax, lie back,
wish the bastard well.

Smashed Glass

There we stood
in our nuptial best
mountains to the left
green velvet the evening air
and my unfortunate thought—
I can't believe it

who invited her
your first wife
Elizabeth   Queen
of French paté
and break-the-bank
imported tile

then came
momentary calm
she was merely a guest
like all the others

yet unlike the others
dressed in her
fresh-from-the-dry cleaners

wedding gown
Park Avenue champagne silk
winking   begging
for one last kiss

you followed that eye
cornflower blue
you took her up on it
a perfunctory (**I** give you that)
dip and peck

then on polished heel
swiveled to face me

for betrayal
I have an excellent ear
I heard the glass splinter
your foot coming down
under my breath
a little groan, my own
private wedding shout

The Champagne Flute

makes us believe
emotion eludes form,
optimism reigns.
If there were words
inside these bubbles
they would read
Gosh, Wow, My
My, What a
Sight.
    The caterer
reveres its design. She
rolls her napkins tight,
plants toothpick chairs
so the fidgety guests
screech to their feet.
Then to the drink—

(the wide-mouth,
hourglass version
kills carbonation.
Enthusiasm fizzles—).

But harnessed,
champagne squeezed
inside a clarinet throat,
and you've caught light in the act
of dawning. We are *for* something, yes!
To the New Year! To Sarah and Jeff! The Revolution!

Honeymoon, Pleasant Hill

Poor sinners, we wandered too far,
lured by those trim Shaker fences
like lace on the good mother's slip.

We slumped in chairs meant to straighten the spine.
Ran our fingers over testicle-shaped finials,
our palms down the Trustees' railing,

smooth as a woman's thigh.
Damn that was good pie, we exclaimed
to the waiter in his Shaker smock.

He cracked a smile (only three survive
in upstate Maine), and kept that
Shaker food coming. Baby

corn, vegetables soaked in lemon oil,
mashed potatoes swollen
around our steak. We tossed and turned the night,

our Shaker beds sheeted too tight—
and woke to labor that zig-zag dance.
First a hum from inside out, then the verse

pitched from brother east to sister west,
against the boards faster, the telltale
thump, heels dug in for good purchase.

Finally, the dousing with an esctatic shout.
(So sure the Shakers were their Godly Version
would bear the future out.)

What Made You Think of That?

He's in the mood,
lifts the covers, skootches in
and with his finger tap tap tap
along my bone. A fresh approach!
though the rhythm's not exactly
sexual, more musical.
Reminds me of something....
but what?

And now I must know *what*—
each thought with its penpal,
one-to-one correlation with the real,
like the cells we smell with,
coded for specific odors. The nose
knows what it's looking for!
So does the baby,
who began to speak by pointing,
its forefinger a little drawbridge,
and the spotted dog outside
ambles its way inside.

(That reminds me: what does it mean
that Native Americans point
with their whole hands?
How many pups is that?)

Oh, back to the question—
it was something I saw earlier,
an at-risk bird-type
shimmying up a telephone pole.
Its namesake was lost
inside my (and Leonardo's)
"excellent darkness"
—a bottomless indoor pool

I didn't even know was there
until it swallowed the word whole.
When my lover and I
relaxed in the shower,
the water released it,
Red Bellied Woodpecker,
though here the correlation is
slightly off, and humorous—
my husband lo and behold
feeling amorous,
his skin scalding pink.
Stop talking so much, he said.

River Mild

Yesterday, I found a bit of pleasure
in the present, in sycamores kissing the river
with one leaf, in their exposed roots
and hidden pebbles. I believed
in continuance as I sat in the boat
which remembered me and still does
though it hangs dry and upside down.
I had forgotten how to steer
but it came to me, the J-stroke,
out of the deep, through my paddle
to the crook of thumb and forefinger.
I floated under vines, over riffles and swells.
I was measured by the angling shadow clock,
the fox-running-along-the-bank clock,
the clock of hunger and exhaustion.
I passed cows in a chain,
then their owner, his wife, son.
I was measured and found fit. My hand
created a tiny wake. I could remove it
and still grow old.

Shared Cup

Chalice in the right hand. Bleached
handkerchief in the left. Still there are those
who never touch the lip. *Dippers* we call them, their wafers
held high like a toe above icy water.
They fear colds or AIDS, are mostly single.
Your clue's in the way they tilt their faces, away.

Or others, shamefully close. A *guzzler*
will lean against your hand, muscle the cup.
Alcoholics are a special case. They
cross their arms over their chest or
when they drink, shake visibly.

Watch out for teenagers who dodge right
then left. Let their parents decide
how much and when. The point
is never to waste a drop, to catch that drop
before it falls onto the secretary's starched collar.

And always wipe around the rim,
though it is gesture, though something intangible
still floats in the wine, enters
each version of bent, holy body.

II.

The Family Afterward

1. Cover Story

One pint is nothing
to a big man—
more than 200 pounds!
The liquor has to travel further,
dilutes, loses potency.
But what do I know?
Here's one thing—
Seagram's is a warm drunk.
Smirnoff or Absolut—cold.
He was smart enough to switch.
No more nastiness; he's
more himself, a gentle,
intelligent teacher
say all the student
evaluations.
You'd think *they'd* notice
if there was a problem.
Their comments are anonymous
and he's always
friendly to suggestions.
Once I asked him to open
a personal checking account,
leave the family funds alone.
Nyquil too, as in
Carver's famous poem.
It seems to have worked...
but I go to bed early,
what do I know?
Just this—he never once
touched the children,

laid a hand on my face
except with a kind of
removed tenderness.
Never smacked up the car,
except in his first
unhappy marriage. But then
he was unhappy.
We are not unhappy.
I am happy.

2. The Rise

We are awash in clutter.
Even the streetlights
flop across our pillows
like wet scarves.
I find a stranger's glove
damp with dew. I find a swelling
on my wrist and, inside the walls,
the scratch of occupation. Oh dear,
the house is shrinking. No, expanding
with eyedroppers and legos,
drywaller's paste
from ten years back.
I climb the stairs
as if they were stones across a stream.
We have 'let things go'
for far too long. We have
watched time back up, pool
until all its edges broke
and we rose as a family
on our very own indoor lake.
My daughter paddles towards me.
Her future is close,
if she could only find it.
A plug somewhere.
Or an old-fashioned, wide open
keyhole.

*Take Miss Rebecca, cashier at the all-night Walgreens. A bottle
a day and a professional "Anything else?" for his right-on-
the-button eleven dollars ninety-five. When he doesn't*

3. Daughter's Villanelle

She saw a man with black hair.
Said to her friend, *Probably my dad,*
face down in the alley. *See? That guy there.*

You paused outside her bedroom door,
startled by what she'd said.
You, a man with clean black hair,

wife, family, flourishing career—
a drink or two now and then. But, *smashed,*
face down in the alley? *Not there*

for his kids, anyone? Why would she compare
the two: your habit not nearly as bad
as the man with the dirty black hair

clothes soaked, chin wedged into the gutter?
You shook your head. *Sad,*
his reddened face, down in the alley... but there's

a chill to her childish swagger:
God, I hope he isn't dead.
Which man with the curly black hair
is lying? Facedown in the alley, there.

show the entire week, she guesses something's up, comes by
the house with chocolate bunnies for the girls. His boss,
dentist, sister, friends Tom and Ann, grandmother, parents,

4. Shot Glass

Either way, he drank—
in defiance, when I
refused him the cash,
square-hipped and loud
on swollen moral ground.
Or in gratitude
if I held my tongue
as he wobbled after
(no use counting)
another two-for-one.

Then, some vacation
the glass appeared—
an upscale shop—
with Depression-style dimples,
fairy tale green.
I bought it for him,
but did not haggle;
the question no longer
was I accessory
but, was I kind.

minister, students—they all watch him with the same
withheld question, trouble in their eyes. // Before cir-
rhosis, the body stages an inelegant fight, venting toxins

5. Contagion

You're outside smoking,
mercury sweating at 90.
The heat doesn't faze—
you like to smoke, its spell
a gray languor down your throat.
My thought, said Pessoa,
has nothing in it,
except that it won't die down.
He knew addiction. You shift
your gaze to my teeshirt, thinned
where my breasts swell.
This too starts something in you.
One touch, one drink,
one cigarette. What I've learned
about your fear of closure!
We have sex and right away
you want to have more.
They say starve a fever,
but that would ruin us.
I don't mind catching
whatever it is you've got.
I slip off my shirt
and move closer.

*through sweat, saliva, tears. Therefore the pillow that smells
like the Bambi Bar, therefore the steering wheel unpleasant to
her touch, the pee in the grass acidic as nail polish remover.*

6. Toddler's Testimony

I wanted to hit him, but exactly I did not.

Ghosts were first. They all died. Then came dinosaurs. Then God made people and I came out of Mom's stomach. I don't know where Dad came from.

Yeah, my tongue keeps opening the door. He can't keep it shut.

Dad. Is he rich? I mean, he has all those teacups.

I was being chased by a tiger. Instead of running, I made a copy of myself, filled it with a motor and sent it down the road. The tiger ran after. I watched from a tree.

Through many dangers, toils, and snails, I have already come.

Therefore the sarcasm, therefore the sympathy, sinking into backyard soil. // Travelers, Inc. has no pity for the self-confessed drinker. They refuse his money,

7. The Next Right Thing

We know the script all too well:
how the clouds will boil
and a lick of wind clip off
our dreams. Sheets
of hail rattle the shingles.
We prepare to move below,
huddle under basement
workbenches,
saving only our souls.
Always in March, this
cleansing, rearrangement,
what we own scattered
to other lives. On the lawn
a housewife finds a bill
from Missouri. Not hers,
but she pays it on time.
She weaves a doormat
from tire scraps and then
repairs the Shaker chair
tossed carelessly to her door.
All without grief, for she
is a good citizen like the thrush,
beak clamped around a shard
of straw. Never a thought
to the ruined nest.
Always a job to do.

*but hold up their sturdy scarlet umbrella over the other
90% still using, incognito, smashing cars, kidneys, mar-
riages, jobs, profits. // There are no true fragments.*

8. Letter from Rehab

Dear one, I'm not allowed to call.
My roommate, the wet-brain,
is supposed to be my wife,
my child, my brother.
The BA in Psychology half my age
is my father. They tell me
J.D.'s been my God for twenty years,
and now I must find the real One
and say...what? *Thank you?*
Well, I am grateful for the food,
the cafeteria racks,
stainless like old lady walkers
but loaded with pies, cakes, puddings—
cigarettes! Free smokes!
Let me tell you, they go down fast.
Twelve steps and I'm
out of here. I confess
I'm struggling with the first.
It's like that old party game,
the one where you close your eyes
and fall helpless blind into
some stranger's hands.

Everything is somehow complete. When the husband goes
South, the wife tips North as far as she can. He's dessert
King. Crème caramel, Hagendaaz with peanuts and

9. Blackout

Blame the alcohol
for lost hours, body
slumped behind the wheel
when so often it's
fear or anger,
what we artlessly call
squirreling—the mind
in crazy footwork, teeth
snapping at the tail, this

powering my car, my
body in Dillard's
shadow, palm on the
fluted door handle
before I realized
it was the wrong mall,
wrong day, foolish
to drive anywhere at all.

fudge sauce. She feels multi-grain cereal with a half-cup
skim milk makes a healthier treat. So too Tofutti ice cream
and Nofun ricotta cheesecake. Soon, a few grains of sand

10. Letter to Rehab

That crucial first year—
Going Inside it's called. I wonder
if you've been warned.
Certainly I have—I'll feel more obviously alone,
whereas up till now the girls and I
have rather enjoyed our solo flight.
Breakfast, school, lunch is the routine.
Then crackers and magazine
cut-outs. Why,
even Queen Victoria
had to be home by eight
so the rest of England could eat!
We've made ourselves comfortable.
I don't want to sound unmerciful
but I wish we could skip ahead a bit
to stage two, where the alcoholic
pays the metaphorical (and literal)
long outstanding bar bill.
Keep your expectations low,
I'm told. *What's furled will grow
into the bouquet of the entire journey.*
I'll watch for that. We miss you dearly.

dragged in by the baby's sandal constitutes a small emer-
gency. Then, the uneaten vegetables, an errant "e" in judg-
ment, mold on a bathroom towel. Her desire for control

12. Derby Glass

And when the last horse trembled in,
scoreboard aflick with Go for Gin,
no one thought of the card game.
Too busy with their tongues
pushing aside that sprig of mint
edged brown with wilt.
Oh the burn
of sugar and corn!
Phil was aslosh. Suzy slurred
her help-the-needy speech, gardenia lurching
from her hat like a swollen
toe.... What's it like
to sniff that paradisal ruin, not even
make it to the gate, nurse a Coke?

grows by the mile as the crow flies, matching precisely his
disdain for it. // You, who thinks addiction is a moral
issue—join the family around the Thanksgiving dinner table,

13. Wife's Chiasmus

And then my husband turned, saying: *Your fury will be the end of me for it only makes me drink. If I die you'll have yourself to blame.* He couldn't blame me when he didn't die, and still he drank, and there was no end to my fury which I turned against my husband.

Sober he said: *Think of the time I wasted drinking. If you add up all the hours, we could have built the finest house in northern Kentucky.* Later, we built a house and threw out the bottles (Kentucky's finest). The hours keeping watch declined. So too the fear his drinking had wasted me.

watch them cock the little finger, bend the elbow, crack a bottle. Follow the wobbly thread through mother half-sozzled by two, sister half-seas by three, brother half-hammered by four.

14. More Q & A

How will we explain it to our friends?
    –Drank so much my wristwatch got heavy.
    Slowed down to let the bridge pass.

No, really, how will we explain it to our friends?
    –Addiction is like art—the less people know about it,
    the more judgmental they become.

So, let's give them an explanation.
    –First the man takes a drink
    Then the drink takes a drink
    Then the drink takes the man.
    How's that?

Tell them what it felt like.
    –Like a tango coat and a jitterbug shawl.

No. Now. What's it like?
    –I'll tell you what it's like.
    Virgin Mary. Bloody Shame.
    Can't bring anything to my lips
    without their hissing—
    he's to blame. Devil.
    Shiftless man.
    This, from educated people.

We don't need that. Or them.
    –You are my eiderdown. My swimming Queen.
    My double dose of valium.

Cousins outside hoisting, twisting, soaking, stitching, gargling
a few. Then my daughter, jumbo in the street like that wall-
eyed, malty, laid-out-in-the-alley stranger, ten years ago.

15. Coda, in Winter

Ridiculous coffee, she thought.
And it's cold. This time
she'll let him know.

But tenderly. Meanwhile
he's decided to let go
his dream
she left the baby alone
to freeze without its jacket.

Anyway by morning
it seems absurd.

Outside the garbage
in brittle plastic bags.
Moon a sliver of ice
stuck to the ceiling.

Remember their first fight,
drinks tossed
in absolute quiet?
Nothing showed.
And then everything.

Friend they read together
comes from *freon*
Old English to love.
So the turn away from love

is a one degree drop
in temperature
that covers the yard
with snow. Good to know

though to them
it's a point of pride—
some rain resists,
goes on softening
a wooden patio,
the snow.

III.

Cupped Hands

Whether left palm over right as in TM
or curved side by side—
human hands are full of leaks. Still,

if we press the fingers close,
by sheer will sealing flesh to flesh,
they will hold something.

—An early disappointment:
a hundred foil-wrapped eggs
in pastel colors. For the taking,

I thought, and began to pluck
from window sills, copper pots,
the dark toes of daddy's socks.

Then the grown-up lesson,
the more I took
the more the eggs resisted

nesting, and capsized, wobbled
away. I ate one tiny handful.
Whether spice drops or wafers

or water carried quickly
over land, we let things slip.
Our hands cupped together

exactly heart-sized;
one hand
alone won't do.

Crossing Myself

Shyly at first,
along with the street faithful
staring at a boy and his crushed
bicycle. Or in courtesy, a tidy one
after grace and before I ate,
a bit of restraint, quick-release.
Lately I've tried it long and deep
over the Jewish half of me,
dubious, self-reliant.
Over the beckoning fingers of my lover
and my embarrassed academic friends.
For them, the forehead touch,
and for him, the tap (two fingers)
just above my sex. It is like sewing
a three foot stitch
that fastens me down, a fly,
but leaves my wings flailing.
Still room to wriggle out
though it might mean damage.
So when I'm all alone,
humbled on the floor
without my glasses on,
I double back to the left shoulder,
fasten a pin there, then the right.
I'm grateful he was half-
human, and at Gethsemani,
pleaded for a little company,
before turning his Jewish face
toward that last kiss.

The Minor Stations

When you walk so early others sleep
—And doesn't nature admire that in you
Though for safety you run your hand along the fence
Then the light's high enough
To decipher a little trail marked *This Way* in stone

The path cuts through woods
Around a reservoir green as Tiffany glass
And up a steel ladder this convenience
Tainting the experience a little
But when you step up you're grateful
For gripping and climbing makes you feel
Your joints and the cold flies up your ankles
Jeans stiffened by snow

A switchback through undergrowth myrtle
Juniper like vitamin-drained vegetables
Then suddenly onto the clear
Crispy grass where the wind picks up
When you walk you remember Emerson's thought
That Pan is the most *continent* of Gods
By this he meant consistent

To signal the trail's end and prompt your
Return there's a limestone cross
Mounted on a pyramid of rose-colored pebbles
Around it hundreds of mementos beads little flags
Passport photographs of lost sons popsicle sticks
Bound by postal rubber bands
A bottlecap filled with apple seeds
Very moving these rookie prayers
This   unmajestic gratitude

The Cure

She bled for twelve years,
enough for twelve women, paid
at least that many physicians.
So when he appeared,
(believers packed tightly
as a school of fish),
she laid down her basket and stared.
He was suspiciously short,
compact, a little breathy.
But the *stories* she had heard—
the infinite picnic wine,
a beggar's luck generously reversed.
Certainly they were right
about the famous cloak, a rich,
buttery color, like almonds.
She inched her way to the front,
past chicken thieves and shepherds,
sick of their thinning burlap,
the filmy brush of human hands.
Her head swam in the heat;
she steadied her knees
under a fruit tree. Finally,
within inches, she reached out.
Who touched my clothes? He demanded
without turning, knowing in himself
that virtue had gone out of him.
It was a commodity, but precious,
on earth only a fixed amount.
His bodyguards scrambled: *He wants an answer,*
who touched his clothes?
but she had already backed off,
feeling better, her issue
miraculously restrained.
Though he didn't reveal it,

he left that spot a lighter man,
his coat beginning to show its age.

Happiness

I think it aims for all of us,
a range of hellos running up
and down the scale. Once in a while
someone like me risks silliness
and actually listens. Once I could tell you
the sound it makes:
tumble of lost pennies in the dryer,
swish of a cotton skirt against pantyhose—
how easy to hear the happiness of others.

I do think it's hungry for my attention
and grows in spite of me, discarding the past
like children's shoes. How else to explain
the sudden tinniness of cicadas
when I returned from the mountains
where an entire *jubilate*
thundered through the trees?
How else to account for the letdown
of home.

I have a notion where it lives.
Something I've read, how happiness
is for the body, suffering for the mind.
Wish I could be one of the physical types
who leave the dinner talk
to chase it across a dewy field,
daisies wilting in their overheated fists.
Their fingers open slowly like a damaged child's;

but shame, shame on me
who thinks happiness is for simple folk,
just because it's easier for them to find,
and they'd rather live than describe it.

Keying Down

to Wren

The book strategizes: wide to narrow.
Abstract to solid down-to-earth.
From the general woods around,
I pluck a five-inch piece of green.
Is the texture succulent?
—my finder questions me.
If so, go here. Is the fern fan-shaped
or mostly round? Divided?
Gradually, the shapeless thing
eases towards the finite:
blade, pinna, pinnule.
I'm focusing in, each tiny part
a place to finger, to rest my foot.
I love the sound of a heel
touching down.
                    Are the spores massed
or asymmetrical? At this
I'm thrown aloft again. What
in God's name are they talking about?
—No spores at all, the naked stipe
and rachis a kind of treachery.
Back into the forest I go
to hunt the fertile stalk
and when I find it (is the sorus smooth,
or scaly brown? My little fern finder,
pocket-sized, 59 pages!),
I know I've reached the floor.
Cinnamon Fern. Osmunda cinnamonia.
Pleased to meet you. Do come in...
its spicy fragrance anchoring me
inside the smear of trees.

Scotoma

Here it comes, like steelwool
or a cluster of pinpricks,
though the visual's being scoured
not her skin and the pain
arrives later. Little by little
what she loves so well
is erased: honeycombed trees,
grass flickering like emeralds, faces
smudged all the way to the forehead,
to their thin crusts of hair.
So it goes for half an hour or so,
till suddenly there's a break,
a bright spot at the center
like the eye on that primordial fish
which was really just a patch
of light sensitive skin.
But now she's afraid to look,
would rather stay in the dark
with the digested trees and grass.
She knew a girl once
with a strange disfigurement,
her mouth perpetually ajar.
Because of sweet lymphatic fluids there,
bees flew in to sting her tongue.
This open spot
is a window to her brain,
an unwelcome consciousness,
as when the moon drops
and we understand
we are food for the stars.

Watch Your Language

Tree, bird, river, house.
When words like dogs
are ill-attended, free
to copulate without conscience,
they turn medium-sized
and brown.

      Before it was a glaze,
celadon was a shepherd
who wore gray-green ribbons.
Before she was a movie,
Elizabeth had breadth
though I loved the pencil-waisted,
poisonous dress.

Permit me my black sun,
my breakfast of foraminifera,
and my hatred of whales

or I too will become a maudlin,
can't-put-my-finger-on-it
drunk and the thing I crave
has the same word

for what I dread.

Cupped Ear

She's a good listener
or so she's been told.
Secrets and songs,
long-winded tales
—their molecules line up
and march right in.
Her kids on the other hand
protect their ears
especially when she complains.
(One evangelist's theory—
very loud rock music
is erotic to the average teenager
and early deafness
their *salvation*.)
The walk is slick
so why must she thrice
remind her mate
to throw down the salt?
Doesn't the ice itself
scold at him?
Men, they say, listen
with half a brain.
But how? And what
are they doing
with the other half?
Calculating, dreaming
a Michigan lake
with fully equipped
hunter's blind?
She would like to see that!
Their aging hound dog
drags its ears in the snow
and yet, misses nothing.
Full plate somersaulting

onto the hardwood,
math book beaning
the trash can.
Even on her testy days
she postpones
all solitary thought,
turns into the sound
her undivided attention.

Dear Growing Teen

Mom walks into your room and trips.
It's probably because:
    a) she's clumsy
    b) she's blind
    c) there's stuff all over the floor

What your room reveals about you!
Brooke Shields, Drew Barrymore,
Fiona Apple, Gwynneth Paltrow.
Hippie chic tie-dye, creative crochet
simply sleek, or glittery glam.

A little extra coverage can be kinda sexy.
What's a girl to do with all those glands?
Tie them, tassle them, add
a hair extender. In short, take defensive action.

Imagine! Pressing your lips together
in an almost perfect way. Fakin' it
so they'll never guess
how many dreams you have per night,

what band broke your heart when they broke up,
what singer's voice goes straight to your soul,
how the actor is handling all this.
You can still sizzle
even if you don't
bare all.

Sleeping on Couches

Because your husband snores and there are birds on your sheets.
It's bad luck to sleep with peacocks.
Because the dog has made a throne of your pillow
and the children are restless inside their bunk beds. Because sleep
is stolen here, like sex on Saturday mornings
with a chair propped against the bathroom door.
Stolen like poems while your husband networks
and the children argue and you are supposed to be crying.
Because events jump around, change course, and the road
hides a nasty curve. Because couches are like sleighs, wagons,
and beds are like windowless cellar rooms.
Because the wealth of your ancestors was in herds
and they lived among strangers, under dirty canvas
and lots of sky. Because this is a parlor, a proper home,
but you have always been disobedient. You are too long
for the cushions and a spring has lodged into your hip,
but you feel drowsy and drop off anyway.
Because you cannot know the future and you need the rest.

Mother/Daughter Truce at the Mote Aquarium

She was hushed by the shark,
sashaying through his greenish realm
like a soft leather glove, his authority
the elegant British kind
(she wants to live in Europe)
and I held my tongue when,
inches from our face,
a seahorse devoured his miniscule,
just-hatched young.
We skipped the snack bar
and headed for the sea urchin,
wedged inside a scallop's shell.
What was it thinking—or does it—
too vast, spiny,
for such a tiny home.
How my little girl had grown,
how she knows me, her brush-off
of treasured girl-to-girl, my motherly best
ignored for good measure.
She bought her own souvenir,
then deliberately dropped it
but amazingly, did not roll her eyes
when I chimed from beside:
"Honey, you dropped your toy,"
though she was too old for either toy
or patronizing tone. What a sight,
manatee like a Good Year blimp,
downed, but live enough
to stuff its dimpled face with lettuce.
Miraculously, she passed up
the obvious comparison
and we both turned smiling
to the very last tank
of moray eels and snapping turtles

and her favorite barracuda,
eye to her eye
suspended near the glass
like a silver stick of dynamite.

Snow Day

I asked for New England,
a long-term white,
but got only a taste,
when overnight
the world became a fancy cake
and I the bride,
hopelessly underdressed
in peacoat and stocking cap.
Courtesan-like yews
nodded as I walked by,
unloosing their coifed,
powdered hair,
as if they knew
it wouldn't last. Still,
the frozen bluegrass
sent little winks my way—
eyelashes brushed with sugar,
And the road's glitter
kept up my hopes, like those
tiny pastel bottles
girls buy for the prom.
But this would be
no cheek to cheek for me,
no gusseted feathers
or lifetime supply of arctic mints.
The heavens had noted my request
and in kindness tossed me
a dozen silver coins
I must spend in one day.

Middle Age

Way too early, a call
from the East. Sun poised on the sill
like a match before striking.
My soft *hello*.

Get your work done, now! my caller
advises. *Trust me, I'm dying in this heat,
it's hours till I'm out of here. Broke*

*a heel on the train, clean off—can't you
just see me limping
all the way through pre-sales?*

Where am I, where are my pants,
why did the phone
hook me from dream
and toss me here

a trout in the grass? Sun
rounds the corner and my skin
overreacts, temperature soaring. Is this natural?
I feel the heat, but not my age.

I meant to thank you, caller says.
When the book arrived, I mean.
Forgot.... Outside, sparrows at the birdbath

seek yesterday's blessing.
Another dozen hackberry leaves
descend out of season. *Are you there?*

Late Evening Love Poem

Don't ask me to stop the dark
slipping into this poem.
I met you in the dark (lines one and three!)
under a Norway pine. Night country.
Lost my flashlight. Pitch
stuck to my bare feet and thighs.
So sure I'd marry a blonde,
but your hair was black.
In Fiji it's a sin to touch a person's hair
but make him a lover
and the taboo disappears.
When kissing we shut our eyes—
inside it's deep mahogany,
licorice, black coffee. Delicious. I was
floating blind
in a year-long gloom.
You were a star in the lit world
and then you fell, a dark
to benefit your poems.
The saying goes, "A man
too good for the world
is no good for his wife." (Yiddish)
We need the dark for seeing inside.
I crashed into you and stars
punctuated my eyelids.
The experts call them "phosphenes."
Scarlet fever will bring them on.
And delirium tremors. Some think
they're explanation for a saint's
visions. Love's door is hinged
with pain. My mother died;
her dying guided me
to you. My favorite sound
is insects in the dark,

rubbing their thighs together. Your jeans
and black silk jacket and shiny
buckled belt. Black makes me thin
and you, hip. How I love
the forties hat that shades your eyes.
I lost my flashlight and bumped into you.
It was an accident. Lucky accident.
Lucky dark.

The Author

Sarah Gorham is the author of *Don't Go Back to Sleep* (1989) and *The Tension Zone*, which was chosen by Heather McHugh as winner of the Four Way Books Award in Poetry (1996). Her poems have appeared widely in such places as *The Nation*, *The Paris Review*, *Grand Street*, *Poetry*, *American Poetry Review*, *DoubleTake*, *Antaeus*, and *Poetry Northwest*, where in 1990, she won the Carolyn Kizer Prize. In 2000, *Prairie Schooner* granted her its "Reader's Choice" Award, and in 2002, she and her husband Jeffrey Skinner were poets-in-residence at the James Merrill House in Stonington, Connecticut. Gorham is co-founder and editor-in-chief of Sarabande Books, Inc. She resides in Louisville, Kentucky.